Useful Machines

Ramps and Wedges

Chris Oxlade

Heinemann Library
Chicago, Illinois

Originated by Ambassador Litho Ltd.
Printed and bound in China by South China Printing Company

07 06 05 04 03
10 9 8 7 6 5 4 3 2 1

Library of Congress Cataloging-in-Publication Data
Oxlade, Chris.
  Ramps and wedges / Chris Oxlade.
      p. cm. -- (Useful machines)
Summary: Describes what ramps and wedges are and how they work,
different types of ramps and wedges and their uses, and other facts
about these simple machines.
Includes bibliographical references and index.
  ISBN 1-4034-3802-1 (lib. bdg.) -- ISBN 1-4034-3803-X (pbk.)
  1. Simple machines--Juvenile literature. 2. Inclined planes--Juvenile
literature. 3. Wedges--Juvenile literature. [1. Inclined planes. 2.
Wedges.] I. Title. II. Series.
  TJ147.O88 2003
  621.8--dc21

2003003788

Acknowledgments
The author and publisher are grateful to the following for permission to reproduce copyright material:
pp. 4, 5, 8, 9, 16, 17, 21, 22, 25 Peter Morris; p. 6 H. Roger/Trip; p. 7 Ted Spiegel/Corbis; p. 10 S. Grant/Trip; p. 11
Alamy Images; p. 12 Lester Lefkowitz/Corbis; p. 13 Layne Kennedy/Corbis; p. 14 Ron Watts/Corbis; p. 15 Farell
Grehan/Corbis; p. 18 Rex Features; p. 19 Sue Cunnigham/SCP; p. 20 Lynda Richardson/Corbis; p. 23 Jonathan
Blair/Corbis; p. 24 Phil Claydon/Eye Ubiquitous/Corbis; p. 26 Dan Guravich/Corbis; p. 27 Humphrey Evans/Sylvia
Corday Photo Library; p. 29 NASA.

Cover photograph by Alamy Images.

Every effort has been made to contact copyright holders of any material reproduced in this book. Any omissions
will be rectified in subsequent printings if notice is given to the publisher.

Some words are shown in bold, **like this.** You can
find out what they mean by looking in the glossary.

Contents

What Are Ramps and Wedges?

ramp

A machine helps us do things. Machines are made up of **simple machines** that work together. Ramps and wedges are simple machines. A ramp is a long **inclined plane,** such as this board.

narrow end

A wedge is like two ramps **joined** together. Here is a wedge made of wood. Two inclined planes come together at the narrow end of the wedge. They form a point.

What Do Ramps and Wedges Do?

We use **pushes** and **pulls** to lift and move things. A ramp makes it easier to move things up or down. This ramp makes it easier to load a truck.

A wedge is a machine that splits things apart. The same push you make on the big end of a wedge is made on the narrow end. These wedges are splitting a log.

How Does a Ramp Work?

A ramp makes it easier to move an object upward. This man needs a lot of **force** to lift a heavy bucket straight up from the ground.

Now the man has lifted the bucket by walking up a ramp. He did not need as much force to move the heavy bucket. It was much easier than lifting the bucket straight up.

Simple Ramps

This ramp is on the back of a tow truck. The car is being **pulled** up the ramp onto the truck. It would be much harder to lift the car straight up onto the truck.

This is a wheelchair ramp. It makes it easy for the person in the wheelchair to get on the bus. Going up a step in a wheelchair would be very tricky.

Path and Road Ramps

Roads are often ramps, too. It is easier for a car to drive along a ramp than a steep road. Highways have gentle ramps. These ramps help keep cars moving fast.

To get the boat out of the river, these people are using a ramp. They tie the boat to a **winch** with a rope. The winch **pulls** the boat up the ramp.

Different Ramp Shapes

Some ramps are built in strange shapes. This **zigzag** street is many ramps put together. They go one way and then the other. It is easier to drive up the zigzag street than straight up the hill.

This ramp goes around in circles. It goes up from one floor to the next in a parking garage. A round ramp takes up less space than a lot of straight ramps.

How Does a Wedge Work?

You can see the wedge shape of this ax head. The downward **force** on the ax is made on the narrow end. This makes it easier for the ax to enter the piece of wood.

The ax is splitting the log. A hammer is being used to **push** the ax down into the log. As the ax head moves down, it pushes the wood farther outward. The log is splitting into two pieces.

Simple Wedges

snowplow

Here are some simple wedges helping people do things. The **snowplow** on this truck is like a wedge. As the truck **pushes** forward, the snowplow pushes the snow to the side.

This man is using a wedge to split a stone. When he hits the wedge, all of the **force** of the hammer comes together on a small part of the stone.

Wedges for Cutting

Tools that cut have **blades.** The sharp edge of the blade is a wedge. This tool is called a **chisel.** The wedge-shaped blade cuts into the wood.

Your front
teeth are like
wedge-shaped
cutting tools.
When you bite
into an apple,
your front teeth
slice through
it, splitting
off chunks.

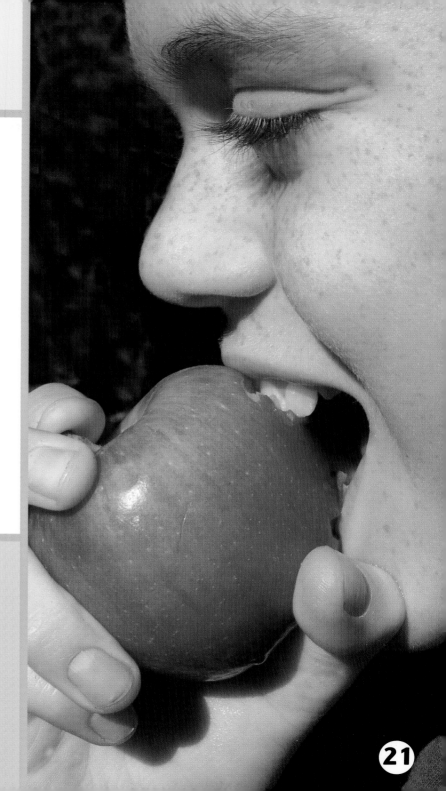

Wedges for Piercing

Needles have sharp points that work like wedges. All of the **force** of this person's hand is **pushing** down on the point of the needle. The needle **pierces** the cloth easily. Nails work this way, too.

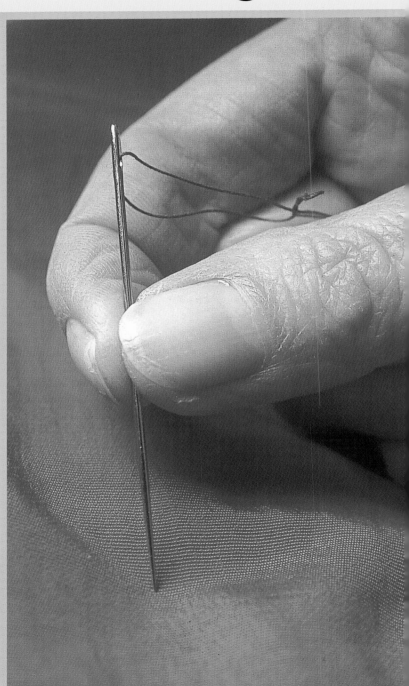

There is a sharp **chisel** on the end of this **jackhammer.** The jackhammer drills down into the road. The chisel works as a wedge. It breaks through the hard **surface** of the road.

Wedges for Holding

chock

chock

Special wedges called chocks stop planes from rolling forward. If the plane's wheels roll and hit the chocks, the chocks are **pushed** against the ground.

This rubber wedge is holding a door open. If you try to shut the door, the wedge will push down on the floor. Wedges like this one change the direction of a push.

Ramps and Wedges in Machines

The **bow** of an icebreaker ship is like a wedge. The **force** of the ship's engines **pushes** at the point of the bow. This makes it easier for the ship to break through the ice.

plow blade

A **plow** has many metal **blades.** Each blade is a wedge. The wedges split up the soil as the tractor **pulls** the plow. The blades also turn over the soil to mix it up.

27

Amazing Ramp and Wedge Facts

- On a **canal** in Belgium, there is a long ramp that carries boats up a hill in a huge tub of water.
- The ancient Egyptians built earth ramps to carry blocks of stone to the tops of the pyramids.
- The space shuttle has to go up a long ramp to its launch pad. The machine that carries the space shuttle up the ramp also keeps it pointing straight up.
- Sports cars and express trains have wedge-shaped fronts that **push** the air out of the way as they speed along.

Rockets go very, very fast. They have wedge-shaped noses. This helps them push through the air on their way into space.

Glossary

blade narrow strip of metal with a sharp edge

bow front end of a ship or boat

canal channel filled with water that boats travel along

chisel tool for cutting and shaping pieces of wood

force push or pull

inclined plane surface or area that slants up or down

jackhammer heavy tool used to break up roads

join put two or more things together

pierce go through a solid material

plow machine that turns over soil in a field

pull   move something closer to you

push   move something away from you

simple machine   machine with no moving parts

snowplow   metal blade that is used to push snow off of a road

surface   top part of something

winch   machine that winds rope or cable. It is used to lift or pull heavy objects.

zigzag   something that moves back and forth sharply as it goes forward

More Books to Read

Douglas, Lloyd G. *What Is a Plane?* Danbury, Conn.: Scholastic Library Publishing, 2002.

Frost, Helen. *What Are Wedges?* Minnetonka, Minn.: Capstone Press, 2001.

Welsbacher, Anne. *Wedges.* Minnetonka, Minn.: Capstone Press, 2000.

Index